SPOT THE DIFFE

Art Masterpiece Mysteries

BOOK 2

DOVER PUBLICATIONS, INC.
Mineola, New York

Planet Friendly Publishing
✓ Made in the United States
✓ Printed on Recycled Paper
Text: 10%   Cover: 10%
Learn more: www.greenedition.org

GREEN EDITION

At Dover Publications we're committed to producing books in an earth-friendly manner and to helping our customers make greener choices.

Manufacturing books in the United States ensures compliance with strict environmental laws and eliminates the need for international freight shipping, a major contributor to global air pollution.

And printing on recycled paper helps minimize our consumption of trees, water and fossil fuels. The text of *Spot the Differences: Art Masterpiece Mysteries, Book 2* was printed on paper made with 10% post-consumer waste, and the cover was printed on paper made with 10% post-consumer waste. According to Environmental Defense's Paper Calculator, by using this innovative paper instead of conventional papers, we achieved the following environmental benefits:

Trees Saved: 8 • Air Emissions Eliminated: 763 pounds
Water Saved: 3,674 gallons • Solid Waste Eliminated: 223 pounds

For more information on our environmental practices, please visit us online at www.doverpublications.com/green

Series Concept and Project Editor: Diane Teitel Rubins
Design Concept: Alan Weller
Designer: Joel Waldrep
Senior Editor: Susan L. Rattiner

Copyright

Bibliographical Note

Spot the Differences: Art Masterpiece Mysteries, Book 2 is a new work, first published by Dover Publications, Inc., in 2010.

International Standard Book Number
ISBN-13: 978-0-486-47300-0
ISBN-10: 0-486-47300-7

Manufactured in the United States by Courier Corporation
47300701
www.doverpublications.com

How well do you truly know the great masterpieces of fine art?

In this book of 25 famous paintings, you will find anywhere from 8 to 17 changes that were made to the originals—from some very obvious differences all the way down to the tiniest little detail. The original painting and the one in which we have made changes are side by side, so you must inspect them both ever so carefully! Just remember: the original work of art always appears on the *left* side! Use your keen observational skills to compare the two pages, and see if you can detect all the differences that appear on the right side of the page. As you discover the differences, remember to keep score by checking the boxes provided on each puzzle page.

Once you have finished strolling through this outstanding gallery of images, you may go to page 54 to check your answers to the puzzles. Try not to peek, though, until you have tried your best to find all the changes! As you go along through the book, you'll learn exciting facts about each painting and its artist. This book is a wonderful and fun introduction to some of the world's greatest works of art.

Giuseppe Arcimboldo
Vertumnus (Portrait of Rudolf II) (1590)

Arcimboldo began his career as a designer of stained glass windows depicting scenes from the lives of the saints.

Arcimboldo was known for his creativity and playful sense of humor. He would cleverly arrange everyday objects to form human faces.

In this painting, Rudolf II is portrayed as the ancient Roman god of orchards, Vertumnus. The likeness was made using only painted images of fruit, flowers, and vegetables.

Royalty greatly admired Arcimboldo. In 1562 he became the court portraitist to Maximilian II and later to Rudolf II, Maximilian's son.

In addition to his work as a portraitist, Arcimboldo was also a court decorator, costume designer, and "event planner," overseeing all of the royal festivities.

Keep Score:
13 Changes

☐ ☐ ☐ ☐ ☐
☐ ☐ ☐ ☐ ☐
☐ ☐ ☐

Frédéric Bazille
Flowers (1868)

Bazille went to Paris in 1862 to study medicine. But in 1864, after failing his exams, he left medical school to study art.

He studied painting at the studio of Charles Gleyre, where he met future Impressionist greats Monet and Renoir. Both men became Bazille's friends and influenced his painting style.

Born to a wealthy family, Bazille was generous with his fellow Impressionists and often shared his studio space and art supplies with them.

Bazille's life was tragically cut short when he was killed in battle during the Franco-Prussian War, just one week before his 29th birthday.

Keep Score:
9 Changes

☐ ☐ ☐ ☐ ☐
☐ ☐ ☐ ☐

Albert Bierstadt
Mountain Landscape (1895) (Detail)

One of the most famous and financially successful landscape painters of the 19th century, Bierstadt was born in Germany and emigrated to America with his family when he was two years old.

Bierstadt was part of the Hudson River School, an informal group of painters whose style involved detailed paintings with romantic, almost glowing light effects.

Mount Bierstadt in Colorado is named in honor of the painter.

Bierstadt was one of the first artists to use a camera to record landscape views. He took countless photographs, which became studies for his massive paintings.

Although best known for his dramatic, panoramic views of the American West, this particular painting portrays the Morteratsch Glacier, in the upper Engadine Valley, Pontresina, Switzerland. It was auctioned in 1990 for close to one million dollars.

Keep Score: **10 Changes** ▫ ▫ ▫ ▫ ▫ ▫ ▫ ▫ ▫ ▫

Pieter Bruegel the Elder
The Peasant Wedding (1567–68)

Bruegel had two sons, Pieter the Younger and Jan. When both boys grew up to be artists, their father became known as Pieter Bruegel the Elder, to distinguish his paintings from those of his sons.

This painting is a realistic record of a Flemish peasants' wedding. The bride is seated in front of the tapestry, but many critics have debated the whereabouts of the groom. Most say that in accordance with Flemish custom, he was not present at the wedding feast. Many others, however, point out one or more possibilities as to the groom's identity. What do you think?

Typical of Bruegel's work, there's lots of activity in this painting and the longer you look at it, the more there is to see. The celebration is set in a barn with a crowd of people at the open door. Platefuls of food are being carried in on an unhinged wooden door. And a hungry musician stares at the food as it is being carried past him.

The artist is known by the nickname "Peasant Bruegel" since he often shows peasants in their everyday lives within his paintings.

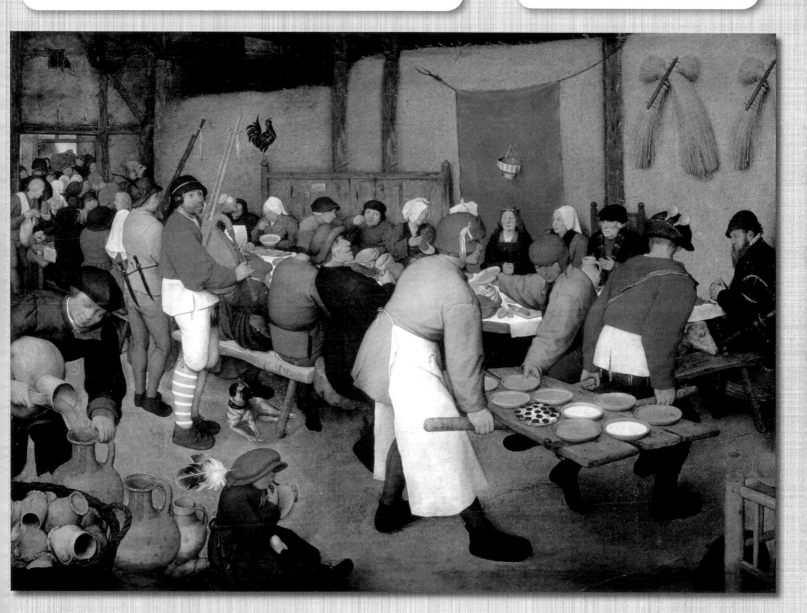

Keep Score: 14 Changes ☐ ☐ ☐ ☐ ☐ ☐ ☐ ☐ ☐ ☐ ☐ ☐ ☐ ☐

Mary Cassatt
The Boating Party (1893–94)

Mary Cassatt was one of only three women—and the only American—ever to join the French Impressionists, a small group of independent French artists.

Although born in America, Mary spent most of her adult life in Paris.

Although she never had any children of her own, Cassatt is perhaps best known for her paintings of mothers and children and the love they share.

The United States Postal Service issued two commemorative stamps in honor of Mary Cassatt. The first, appearing in 1966, was a five-cent stamp picturing this painting. The second, issued in 1988, was a twenty-three-cent stamp of her portrait.

Sadly, Cassatt lost her sight from cataracts in 1914 at the age of 70 and had to give up painting.

Keep Score: 12 Changes ☐ ☐ ☐ ☐ ☐ ☐ ☐ ☐ ☐ ☐ ☐ ☐

Paul Cézanne
The Kitchen Table (1888–90)

Cézanne believed that everything in the world was made up of a sphere, a cone, a cylinder, or a cube. He began many of his works using these basic shapes.

This painting has hung in three famous museums in Paris—the Louvre, the Jeu de Paume, and the Musée d'Orsay, where it resides today.

Cézanne is often described as "the Father of Modern Art."

Keep Score: 10 Changes ☐ ☐ ☐ ☐ ☐ ☐ ☐ ☐ ☐ ☐

Ralph Earl
Elijah Boardman (1789)

Although American by birth and the son of a colonel in the Revolutionary Army, Ralph Earl sided with the British and fled to London, where he stayed until two years after the end of the Revolutionary War.

This painting portrays Elijah Boardman, one of the artist's most prominent and generous patrons. An impressive, full-length, life-sized work (almost 7 feet high!), it shows the richly dressed New Milford, Connecticut, merchant in his store, where he sold plain and patterned fabrics.

During his time in jail, Earl created a portrait of Elizabeth Schuyler, the wife of America's first Secretary of the Treasury, Alexander Hamilton.

Earl was put in debtors' prison in New York City in 1786. Interestingly, the very people who put him in jail—the mayor, trial recorder, and sheriff—soon became his patrons. They ordered and paid for portraits in an effort to help Earl get the money necessary to gain his freedom.

Elijah Boardman was a U.S. Senator from Connecticut.

Keep Score:
14 Changes

☐ ☐ ☐ ☐ ☐
☐ ☐ ☐ ☐ ☐
☐ ☐ ☐ ☐

Jean-Honoré Fragonard
A Young Girl Reading (1776)

Fragonard painted in the Rococo style, also referred to as "French style" art. This style of painting was highlighted by soft pastel colors and playful designs.

Fragonard was known for the variety of his brushstrokes. In this painting, each texture is painted using a different stroke—heavy and thick for the girl's dress, light and loose for the pillows, and scratched into the white paint with the wooden tip of the brush for the girl's collar.

In 1752, Fragonard won the Prix de Rome award. The prize was a scholarship that paid for him to study painting in Rome.

Known as one of France's most significant painters of the 18th century, Fragonard was one of the favorites in the courts of both King Louis XV and King Louis XVI.

X-rays have shown that the canvas of this work originally contained an image of a man.

Keep Score:
8 Changes

☐ ☐ ☐ ☐
☐ ☐ ☐ ☐

Thomas Gainsborough
The Blue Boy (1770)

The Blue Boy, one of Gainsborough's best-known paintings, is believed to portray Jonathan Buttall, the son of a wealthy British merchant and friend of the artist.

The boy in the painting is dressed in a costume dating about 140 years *before* the portrait was painted. Gainsborough so admired the paintings of Anthony van Dyck that he copied everything from the pose to the clothing of the Flemish artist's works.

In 1774 London, Gainsborough's subjects included many of the rich and famous, such as King George III and Queen Charlotte.

After 150 years in Britain, *The Blue Boy* was sold to American railway pioneer Henry Edwards Huntington for $728,800, a then-record price for any painting (that's almost $8 million today!). Before its departure to California in 1922, the Gallery's director scrawled the farewell words "Au revoir" and his initials on the back of the painting.

Gainsborough was often late delivering paintings to his patrons. This prompted him to once write "painting and punctuality mix like oil and vinegar."

Keep Score:
8 Changes

Paul Gauguin
Tahitian Women (1891)

Gauguin had a successful career as a stockbroker when he took up painting as a hobby.

This painting typifies Gauguin's style of painting using simplified designs, bold splashes of color, and bright streaks of unmixed paint.

A restless man, Gauguin traveled and worked in the French regions of Brittany and Provence as well as the South and Central Americas. In 1891, he moved to the French colony of Tahiti in search of an exotic life in "paradise." He spent all but two of the remaining years of his life in the South Seas.

Original Gauguin paintings are rarely found for sale. If they are, the asking price could be close to $40 million.

Keep Score: 14 Changes ☐ ☐ ☐ ☐ ☐ ☐ ☐ ☐ ☐ ☐ ☐ ☐ ☐ ☐

Vincent van Gogh
Self-Portrait (1889)

The artist painted a total of 35 self-portraits at regular intervals throughout his life. As he later wrote in a letter to his brother: "If I succeed in painting the colors of my own face, which is not without its own difficulties, then I should be able to paint those of other men and women."

Van Gogh created his most famous work, *Starry Night*, while staying in an asylum in Saint-Rémy-de-Provence, France.

Van Gogh sold only one painting in his entire lifetime—*Red Vineyard at Arles* (now in the Pushkin Museum, Moscow).

Van Gogh produced all of his work (some 900 paintings and 1,100 drawings) during a period of only 10 years. After struggling with mental illness for many years, he committed suicide in 1890. His fame grew rapidly after his death, especially following an art show of 71 of his paintings in Paris in 1901 (11 years after his death).

Van Gogh wrote more than 700 letters to his brother, Theo. The letters, published after his death, provide a written record of the artist's life.

Keep Score:
8 Changes

Francisco Goya
Don Manuel Osorio Manrique de Zuñiga (1788)

Francisco Goya was born in a village in northern Spain. His father was a gilder (an artist who applies thin sheets of gold to paintings) who apprenticed his son to a local painter.

The pet magpie (a bird that belongs to the same family as crows, ravens, and jays) is actually holding the painter's calling card in its beak.

This painting shows contradictions that can be found in many of Goya's works of art. The focus is on a seemingly happy child in a bright red suit. But the cats in the background, staring intently at the child's pet bird, suggest that danger is nearby.

After studying art in Italy, Goya settled in Madrid, Spain, where he painted designs (called cartoons) for the Royal Tapestry factory. Eventually he became a court painter to a line of Bourbon kings: Carlos III, his son Carlos IV, and his grandson, Fernando VII.

A serious illness in 1792 left Goya permanently deaf.

Keep Score:
8 Changes

☐ ☐ ☐ ☐
☐ ☐ ☐ ☐

Edward Hicks
Peaceable Kingdom (1834)

A Pennsylvania sign painter and Quaker preacher, folk artist Edward Hicks is thought to have painted between 60 to 100 different versions of *Peaceable Kingdom*.

In the background of this painting, William Penn is pictured with others making a treaty with the Leni-Lenape Indians.

The *Peaceable Kingdom* paintings were Hicks' interpretations of the Biblical passage from Isaiah 11 that all men and beasts live in harmony. The theme appealed to his fellow Quakers, to whom he gave most of these paintings as gifts.

A self-taught artist, Hicks adopted a single theme in his paintings and refined and repeated it throughout his lifetime.

Keep Score: 11 Changes ☐ ☐ ☐ ☐ ☐ ☐ ☐ ☐ ☐ ☐ ☐

Édouard Manet
The Fife Player (1866)

Although sometimes called an Impressionist, Manet is now regarded as a Realist who influenced and was inspired by the Impressionist painters of the 1870s.

Manet's contemporary subjects and bold manner with paints inspired future Impressionists, although Manet never exhibited with them.

This painting was refused admission to an important art exhibition in Paris in 1866.

Art critics believe that Manet might have based the piper boy on several different models. However, the piper's face resembles that of Victorine Meurent, a girl who appears in *The Street Singer* and other Manet paintings.

Keep Score:
8 Changes

☐ ☐ ☐ ☐
☐ ☐ ☐ ☐

Grandma Moses (Anna Mary Robertson)
A Beautiful World (1948)

Without any formal art training, American folk painter Anna Mary Robertson Moses, better known as Grandma Moses, spent most of her life as a farmer's wife in upstate New York before painting her first picture.

Grandma Moses first created embroidery pictures, but when arthritis made needlepoint too painful, she turned to painting instead.

The governor of New York proclaimed September 7, 1960, to be "Grandma Moses Day" in honor of her 100th birthday. Grandma Moses lived to be 101 years old.

Edvard Munch
The Scream (1893)

The Scream, sometimes referred to as *The Cry*, is often considered the first Expressionist painting.

In an entry in his journal, Munch described the vision that inspired his most famous painting: "I was walking along the road with two friends. The sun was setting. I felt a breath of melancholy— Suddenly the sky turned blood-red. I stopped, and leaned against the railing, deathly tired—looking out across the flaming clouds that hung like blood and a sword over the blue-black fjord and town. My friends walked on—I stood there, trembling with fear. And I sensed a great, infinite scream pass through nature."

Many scientists think that the "blood-red" sky that Munch witnessed on that fateful night was a volcanic sunset caused by the massive 1883 eruption of the Krakatoa volcano in Indonesia, one of the worst volcanic eruptions in history.

After his death, a collection of more than 1,000 paintings, 4,500 drawings, and over 15,000 prints were discovered behind locked doors in his home.

Keep Score:
8 Changes

☐ ☐ ☐ ☐
☐ ☐ ☐ ☐

Pierre-Auguste Renoir
Luncheon of the Boating Party (1880–81)

Renoir began his artistic career in his early teens painting designs on china in a Paris porcelain factory.

This painting depicts a group of Renoir's friends sharing a meal and conversation at a restaurant outside of Paris, France. The painter and art patron, Gustave Caillebotte, is seated at the lower right. Renoir's future wife, Aline Charigot, is the woman seated in the front wearing a flowered hat and holding a dog.

Renoir was part of the Impressionist group of painters. He often painted outdoors to show the light of the sun as realistically as possible.

Renoir was inspired to become an artist after a visit to the Louvre in Paris when he was about nine years old. Before he died, he was able to visit the museum and see his own paintings hanging there!

During the last 20 years of his life, Renoir was so crippled with arthritis that he found it difficult to paint. By strapping a brush to his hand, he was able to continue doing what he loved.

Keep Score: 10 Changes ☐ ☐ ☐ ☐ ☐ ☐ ☐ ☐ ☐ ☐

Henri Rousseau
Paysage Exotique (1910)

Rousseau did not begin to paint until he was almost 40 years old. He was an untrained, completely self-taught artist.

He is best known for his exotic jungle scenes. Visits to the zoos and botanical gardens in Paris provided the inspiration for his imaginative art.

Rousseau held a job with the Paris Customs Office when he took up painting as a hobby. He retired from his job early, at age 49, so that he could devote his time entirely to art.

There are more than twenty jungle paintings, almost all of which are large in size.

Peter Paul Rubens
The Duke of Lerma (1603)

Widely respected and extremely successful, Peter Paul Rubens was a celebrity artist of his time. He was also a scholar and a diplomat, who was trusted with delivering important messages between the rulers of Spain and England.

This painting of a powerful political figure on horseback exhibits many elements of Rubens' Baroque style—a bold, dramatic scene with elaborate ornamentation and lots of movement.

In 1630, he was knighted by Charles I of England for his role in negotiating the peace treaty that ended the Anglo-Spanish War.

Rubens employed teams of skilled assistants who helped him complete assignments. He created the initial sketches and added final touches and the assistants did all of the steps in between. His studio was so large that Rubens built a gallery where spectators could view the works-in-progress, as if they were in a theater.

Rubens built a large Italian Renaissance-style house with classical arches and sculptures that served as both his home and workshop. It was restored after 1937, and is now a public museum in Antwerp, Belgium.

Keep Score:
8 Changes

John Singer Sargent
Mrs. Carl Meyer and Her Children (1896)

Known for his glamorous portraits of British and American high society at the turn of the century, Sargent's long list of rich and famous clients helped to make him the leading portrait painter of his generation.

This painting, of the socialite Adele Meyer and her children, Elsie Charlotte and Frank Cecil, is one of Sargent's most famous portraits.

The son of prosperous parents, Sargent had an international upbringing. The artist William Starkweather once described Sargent as "an American born in Italy, educated in France, who looks like a German, speaks like an Englishman, and paints like a Spaniard."

Sargent painted a series of three portraits of the famous author Robert Louis Stevenson. The second, *Portrait of Robert Louis Stevenson and His Wife* (1885), was one of his best known. It sold for $8.8 million in 2004 to a Las Vegas casino owner.

Keep Score:
8 Changes

☐ ☐ ☐ ☐
☐ ☐ ☐ ☐

Georges Seurat
A Sunday Afternoon on the Island of La Grande Jatte (1884–86)

This painting is one of the most famous and frequently reproduced works of art in the world. Since it was donated to the Art Institute of Chicago in 1926, tens of millions of people have come to visit it.

Curiously, the only figure that peers at the viewer is that of a young girl in the center of the painting. All other figures and pets appear to be either gazing at the river, the sky, or each other.

Seurat completed seven very large paintings and about 500 smaller ones during his brief lifetime. He created this masterpiece at the age of 26 and died soon after at age 31 from an infection.

Seurat invented a technique of applying small dots, or points, of color to a canvas in order to create variations of shade without losing any of the color's brilliance. Today, this technique is known as Pointillism.

This painting is an impressive size . . . approximately 6 feet 10 inches high and over 10 feet long. It took Seurat two years to complete!

Keep Score: 17 Changes ☐ ☐ ☐ ☐ ☐ ☐ ☐ ☐ ☐ ☐ ☐ ☐ ☐ ☐ ☐ ☐ ☐

James Tissot
Holyday (The Picnic) (c. 1876)

This painting is set in Tissot's garden. The colonnade and pool in the background appear in other paintings and etchings by Tissot.

Friends and professional models posed for this painting in a variety of costumes from Tissot's own studio wardrobe.

During the first half of Tissot's life, he concentrated on modern, everyday life scenes, depicting fashionable men and women engaged in leisure activities such as boating, picnics, and horseracing.

During the second half of Tissot's artistic life, he became focused on religion and created what was to become known as Tissot's Bible. His 865 watercolors covering the life of Christ were highly praised.

Henri de Toulouse-Lautrec
Dance at the Moulin Rouge (1890)

As a child, Toulouse-Lautrec broke both of his legs in accidents that left him crippled for life. While recovering from his injuries, he began to paint.

This painting is set in the Moulin Rouge, a famous nightclub in Paris, France.

Toulouse-Lautrec loved the glamorous nightlife of Paris and frequently visited the city's dance halls, cafés, theaters, and the circus. It was at these places that he found his subjects: singers, dancers and clowns. He painted these entertainers using flowing, expressive lines full of movement and energy.

Toulouse-Lautrec was the first painter to design advertisements, and some of his most famous works are the posters he created for theatrical shows, exhibitions, and celebrated performers.

The dancers at left center are dancing the "cancan," a lively dance that first appeared in Parisian dance halls in the 1830s.

Keep Score: 10 Changes ☐ ☐ ☐ ☐ ☐ ☐ ☐ ☐ ☐ ☐

Diego Velázquez
Las Meninas (1656)

Clearly the center of attention, five-year-old Princess Margarita is shown in a golden light while the figures around her are painted in shadow.

This painting, perhaps his best known, was the artist's last great work.

This painting also includes a self-portrait, since Velázquez painted himself painting a picture. The artist is the man standing behind the large easel holding a palette in his left hand and a paintbrush in his right hand. Look closely and you can see a reflection of the King and Queen in the mirror on the back wall.

In 1623, Spain's King Philip IV appointed Velázquez the official painter to the royal household. He and his family lived in comfort in the palace from that time on.

Velázquez never titled this painting. After he died, it became known as Las Meninas, which means "The Maids of Honor." This refers to the young girls chosen to serve the princess and live in the palace.

Keep Score:
12 Changes

James Abbott McNeill Whistler
Arrangement in Grey and Black No. 1 (Portrait of the Artist's Mother) (1871)

Although born in America, Whistler spent most of his life in London and Paris.

Whistler's etching *Black Lion Wharf* is hung on the wall in the background of this painting.

In 1934, the U.S. Post Office issued a three-cent stamp engraved with a stylized image of "Whistler's Mother" accompanied by the slogan, "In Memory and in Honor of the Mothers of America."

Whistler's mother, Anna McNeill Whistler, posed for the painting while living in London with her son.

Keep Score: 9 Changes ☐ ☐ ☐ ☐ ☐ ☐ ☐ ☐ ☐

Pages 4–5   Giuseppe Arcimboldo
Vertumnus (Portrait of Rudolf II)

- Onion Changed to Apple
- Grape Added
- Sunflower Added
- Yellow Flower Added
- Chili Pepper Added
- White Flower Added
- Artichoke Added
- Leek Removed
- Onion Added
- Cherry Tomato Added
- Banana Added
- Cherry Added
- Plum Added

Pages 6–7   Frédéric Bazille
Flowers

- Calla Lily Added
- Red Flower Added
- Vase Color Changed
- Stripe Added to Vase
- Table Leg Removed
- Parrot Added
- Orange Flower Removed
- Rose Added
- Lizard Added

Pages 8–9   Albert Bierstadt
Mountain Landscape (Detail)

- Airplane Added
- Cloud Added
- Branch Removed
- Tree Added
- Horse & Rider Added
- Buffalo Skull Added
- Rock Added
- Rattlesnake Added
- Grizzly Bear Added
- Campfire Added

Pages 16–17 Ralph Earl
Elijah Boardman

- Blue Cloth Extended
- Quill Pen Removed
- Green Cloth Lowered
- Hanging Cloth Removed
- Doorknob Sign Added
- Duck Added
- Book Upside Down
- Book Removed
- Shoe Buckle Removed
- Sock Pattern Added
- Axe Added
- Button Added to Sleeve
- Vest Pocket Added
- Wall Panel Added

Pages 18–19 Jean-Honoré Fragonard
A Young Girl Reading

- Butterfly Added
- Picture Added to Book
- Finger Removed
- Teacup Added
- Sleeve Cuff Removed
- Flowers Added
- Pattern Added to Drapes
- Pearl Earring Added

Pages 20–21 Thomas Gainsborough
The Blue Boy

- Moon Added
- Hair Removed
- Jacket Closed
- Tree Removed
- Dog Added
- Feather Removed from Hat
- Bow at Knee Removed
- Castle Added

Pages 22–23 Paul Gauguin
Tahitian Women

- Cloud Added
- Flower Added Behind Ear
- Water Color Changed
- Crab Added
- Leaf Pattern Added
- Flower Pattern Removed
- Shell Added
- Bracelet Added
- Box Removed
- Flower Added on Sand
- Foot Removed
- Dress Color Changed
- Parrot Added
- Red Bow Removed

Pages 24–25 Vincent van Gogh
Self-Portrait

- Van Gogh's *Starry Night* Added
- Glasses Added
- Earring Added
- Beard on Cheek Removed
- Shirt Removed
- Vest Color Changed
- Button Added
- Flower Added

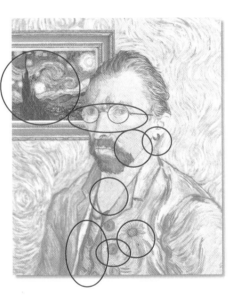

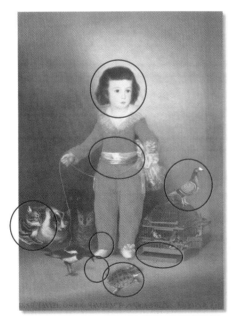

Pages 26–27 Francisco Goya
Don Manuel Osorio Manrique de Zuñiga

- Head Turned
- Sash at Waist Narrowed
- Cat Added
- Bow Removed from Shoe
- Paper Removed from Beak
- Turtle Added
- Drawer Opened
- Pigeon Added

Pages 28–29 Edward Hicks
Peaceable Kingdom

- Bird Added
- Tree Color Changed
- Elephant Added
- Ox's Horn Removed
- Man Removed
- Chicken Added
- Girl Removed
- Cloth Removed
- Calf Removed
- Tiger's Tail Removed
- Birdhouse Added

Pages 30–31 Édouard Manet
The Fife Player

- Tassel Added
- Finger Moved
- Button Added to Sleeve
- Drum Added
- Shoe Color Changed
- Stripe Added to Pants
- Button Removed from Jacket
- Flute Lengthened

Pages 32–33 Grandma Moses
A Beautiful World

- Land Added
- Roof Color Changed
- Horse Added
- Girl Added
- Tree Removed
- Stream Added
- Duck Added
- Window Added
- Chimney Added
- Woman Added
- Tree Added
- Boat Added
- Hot Air Balloon Added

Pages 34–35 Edvard Munch
The Scream

- Mountain Added
- Boat Added
- Person Added
- Board Removed
- Mouth Changed
- Arm and Hand Removed
- Lake Extended
- Bird Added

Pages 36–37 Pierre-Auguste Renoir
Luncheon of the Boating Party

- Sleeve Added
- Watch Added
- Bottle Removed
- Cake Added
- Tattoo Added
- Stripe Added to Hat
- Man Removed
- Dress Color Changed
- Awning Flap Removed
- Pole Removed

Pages 38–39 Henri Rousseau
Paysage Exotique

- Orange Removed
- Plant Added
- White Flower Added
- Pink Flower Added
- Ostrich Added
- Monkey Added
- Zebra Added
- Bird Added
- Leaf Removed

Pages 46–47 James Tissot
Holyday (The Picnic)

- Man Removed
- Knothole in Tree Added
- Flower in Hat Added
- Slice of Cake Removed
- Blanket Stripe Added
- Fork Added
- Silver Cup Added
- Blanket Color Changed
- Seal Added
- Bird Added
- Arm Moved
- Hat Stripe Removed
- Lapel Flower Color Changed
- Toy Boat Added
- Pillar Removed

Pages 48–49 Henri de Toulouse-Lautrec
Dance at the Moulin Rouge

- Pillar Added
- Window Color Changed
- Man in Red Turned
- Woman's Leg Moved
- Stripe Removed from Pants
- Skirt Color Changed
- Hat Added on Floor
- Coat Lengthened
- Light Fixture Added
- Man Removed

Index